FINESTRA'S WINDOW

FINESTRA'S WINDOW

poems by Patricia Corbus

Off the Grid Press

Somerville, Massachusetts

ACKNOWLEDGMENTS

Many of the poems in this book have been previously published, as follows:

Alabama Literary Review: A Quiet Walk
The Chariton Review: Dead American Boy, The Pilot, The Woodchuck's Song
The Cincinnati Review: Luncheon at the Club, Message from Space, Drinking Fog Ceremony
Conversation Pieces: Poems that Talk to Other Poems, selected by Kurt Brown and Harold Schechter, Everyman's Library, Borzoi, Alfred A. Knopf, 2007: The Blue-Eyed Wife
Cottonwood: Warning for a Daughter
Deus Loci, the International Lawrence Durrell Journal: Trolling for Poets (finalist, White Mice Poetry Contest)
88: A Journal of Contemporary American Poetry: A Meeting of the Historical Society, She Stares into Space
Georgia Review: Your Horoscope Today
Gettysburg Review: In the Audience
Green Mountains Review: Rowing to Quintana Roo, Chameleon, Midnight Sortie, Something about Space which Saddens, Sailing at Sunset (nominated for the Pushcart Prize; included in *25th Anniversary Poetry Retrospective)*
Hotel Amerika: Music from the Cave, The Seamstress
Kestrel: Buried Statue, Movie with a Dead Poet
The Madison Review: Accomplished Dreamers
The Main Street Rag: Marionette (I), The Wedding
Midwest Quarterly: Cloud Study
New Letters: The Blue Flash
New Ohio Review: A Simple Request
Nimrod International Journal: Astronomy, That One (Honorable Mention, Pablo Neruda Prize)
Notre Dame Review: Pimpernel, One Fabulous Bird, Turnback, Solstice, Rushing Heaven, After the Swan
Rhino: the Poetry Forum: Concerning Form
Sonora Review: The Unmixing
The South Carolina Review: Terms
Southern Humanities Review: More Air, More Water
The Wallace Stevens Journal: Cold Poem, The Crazy Giant, To Him and Him, Three A.M.
Witness: About Fish

Profound thanks to Muriel Nelson and Martha Zweig, to Nathan Bezner, Lili Corbus Geer, and Burton Corbus, as well as to the woman who read to me, the man who slipped poems under my door, and the teachers who threw open so many windows, then flew away—Donald Justice, Aga Shahid Ali, and Steve Orlen.

Off the Grid Press
24 Quincy Street
Somerville, MA 02143
http://offthegridpress.net

Front cover: Aimee Belanger, *80/100*, watercolor on paper, 12 x 9 inches, 2012. Collection of the artist.

Printed by Cushing-Malloy, Inc., Ann Arbor, Michigan. Book design by Michael Alpert.

ISBN: 978-0-9778429-8-8

CONTENTS

1.

2.

3.

4.

FINESTRA'S WINDOW

1.

Open the sky-box, Uncle,
and take out the marionette.
He wants to breathe,
he wants to dance
with a girl, someone tender.
He is tired of being wood,
rigid, requiring another's will.
He wants to waltz
into the forest, his old home,
and become a man,
sit beside his brothers
the trees, and kiss the girl.

DRINKING FOG CEREMONY

In pearly clouds
called fog we sit
on unseen chairs

and sip strong tea

made of cobwebs.
Under the stars,
old red, young blue,

we watch races,

headlights, crashes.
We call it home.
Cat weaves himself

among us, now

sniffing tea, now
sniffing air. Not
impressed.—Gone.

Spider makes tents

on dripping grass.
Come, homebody
and voyager.

We stay, we go.

The sun drives off
billowing mists,
but still we drink

transparent cups

of milky thread.
Magnolia tree
glistens and clacks.

Windows open.

CONCERNING FORM

What is a shell
but a limestone
pen, the record
of a life lived,
executing
its whorls, turning
on the ocean
floor, laying down
shadows of moods,
foods and colors—
monument, home?
Not like the dawn,
that animal
without a shell
crawling over
the horizon.

What use are forms
but to expose
what already
exists, unseen—
invisible
bubble, squirming
inside a taut,
nacreous skin
of spreading dew?

Architecture,
deep skeleton
and anchorage,
I cling to you,

who hold me here,
formless, skinless,
green and growing.
I can keep none
of your children
from flying home

—Don't sail me
without a ship,
nameless, naked,
into your sky,
that meaningless,
leafless,
forest of foam.

ABOUT FISH

Something is going on with me about fish.

When I see them, still trying to breathe,
left by fishermen on Siesta Bridge
    (once I watched one being filleted,
            still heaving with sides no longer there)—

I feel unbearable pity and horror,
    although I could not touch a fish to save it.

    Now is it too late for you to live?
            Is it too late *now* for you to live?
                    Is it too late for you to live *now*?
—At what precise point is it really too late?

When I come upon the ad in a newspaper—
a big fish doubled up in a brandy snifter—
I close the page fast, and do not let it touch me.

I hate menus that say "battered" fish.
I hate clothes, dishes, jewelry with images of fish.

A poem I read about the teacup of an eye
staring out of a net still haunts and revolts me.
(Don't get the idea that I am that fish. I'm not.)

I like the smell of the Gulf.
I myself smell like a fish.

I remember being carried by my father down to our boat,
and waking hours later in the cabin, rocking in the Gulf

—And then the rhythmic thumps of a fish, a tarpon
my father had just caught, being swung hard,
Bang, Bang, Bang against the side of the boat
(To stun it? Kill it?)

I lay in confusions of filtered light,
happy to be near my father, hoping the fish was a big one,
flashing silver flames in the dawn, scales flying.

I think that the thousands of fish my father killed
are beginning to take their revenge on me.

I don't think I will eat fish again.

I want what is deep and alien to remain deep and alien.
To be left alone.

ACCOMPLISHED DREAMERS

The dead begin as dolls
lolling in wintry nobility,
but collect and release
billowy clouds
until they regain the fluidity
of their lives—finally
spattering forgiveness
like rain on concrete.
Take for example P...,
so long under slab,
now so fully loved by F...,
who heretofore hated
her weakness (hot heart,
could not drive in traffic,
fish, or chair committees).
Easily distraught, easily
taught what she so easily
forgot, easily silenced
and led to tears, now she
is dearly loved, indispensible
as he had been to her.
Disgusted, once he watched
her mouth the words "plinth,"
"wicket," "alcazar."
—Tonight, he shapes and sounds
out loud, "transvaal," "chowchow,"
"finestra," sending them
circling like bees to the tops
of live-oak trees, and feels
a light breeze carry her

slowly home to him.

THE CRAZY GIANT

Leave the gray plate of clouds overhead,
the farms pigged and goated, and follow a string
of taut light into the crazy giant's house

where, stupid and cunning, he hides in a closet—
but which one?—with his axe, hoping that nothing
can hurt a useless thing, turn it into farmer

or fireman, no cracked tree into coffins or pencils.
He used to dream that an enormous collie
and he were tussling with Granny's pink girdle,

but lately dreams he is a green mouse, the Wizard
of Chartreuse, or worse luck, a living holly
squashed between two panes of glass. Heavens,

sometimes he looks into the mirror for so long
that he trembles and runs, suspecting the fun
of hiding less than the horror of being found.

He smells the freshest smell of nightsoil now,
of something digesting wood. How he wants to run
to all the hamlets in town, flying some flame-

colored banner over his head—but he and Prince
bark at winter sundogs and keep on running and
running along what enchanted old chain-link fence?

POWER OF WINTER

The lake wrinkles, clears its forehead, frowns, reflects. I try
to placate it, pour nickels into its depths, shining their slow tilt down.
I lie upon it, face down, searching its hidden face, our magic spots
touching. I skim its surface, slippery as metal, toward Milwaukee,
wooden slivers of light fruiting, then fluting.

A pair of rats swims with me, silver bubbles, baroque pearls,
rising from their mouths. The day above my head, blue, blue above
that, then black, foaming with anti-matter, dark matter, no matter.
Arms in and out of water, the surf not individual waves, just roar.

I married her in autumn, when her sparkles were less frivolous,
when she was more mature, had known sorrow. Yet winter's cold
hand fell upon us like a spirit that chills the conversation in a
restaurant. Untellable secrets, her colossal privacy, that sort of thing.

The fish on the weather vane whirred and whirred in the month
of water, February, when she no longer spoke to me. In spring
I remembered that she springs from high north rocks that must never
be named. Sometimes I catch a glimpse of the child she had by me,
a boy shaped like a cloud.

I am the haunter of the shore, following my floating boy.

MORE AIR, MORE WATER

Last night on the top of Delectable Mountain,
looking at a twenty-minute sundog over Mirror Lake,
I didn't feel like apologizing any more
that I am happy, my life again swept up by cable car.

Surely your life has had its moments—
stoking coal on an ore boat during the war, Lake Michigan
muttering up another widow-making storm—
hooking silver tarpon while Florida still had them,
the morning simple as a deep, searching kiss.

Chased, running booze from Cuba, you ditched the boat
in mangroves, hitchhiked home, and the next week
bought back your boat in Tampa from the Feds.
Those were the morning days. They did not graduate to noon.

Bait that stayed too long in the bucket, never released,
for fifty years you have not caught your breath.
You live in me like a swallowed hook,
strangler fig squeezing my palm tree,
for whom I shrink to give more air, more water—

What a long suicide! Your head being blown off slowly,
and I never able to stop you—or tear my eyes away.

THE BLUE-EYED WIFE

When the buzzards turned my husband into a buzzard,
  I stood in the fields and watched them glide.
Their pinions caressed the white skin of my throat.
  Their strength circled, tilted, and slid into me
Until we hung there like kites in a gorge of air.

And then I was freed from the duties of milking,
  Of feeding the old ones now the young ones are gone.
Their faces were hooded with crimson ribbons,
  And their bones were thrown in the marly loam
Of Borrow Pit, turning white in a white leprous foam.

He comes at the dead of night to watch me breathe—
  When my eyelids quiver, I am dreaming of flight.
Then shadows move and long wings double—he blots
  Out the stars, overshadows my feathers. I shudder,
My eyes black with a hunger that can never be eased.

TROLLING FOR POETS

I first snagged the silver-buckled high hats
   of those right with God and man, and went on
      to hook the broidered coats of those who flew

the scarves of their own Renaissance on wrists
   and ankles. I chummed for those easy to see
      from the deck, who travel under the great ships

and eat refuse dumped from them. But the fish
   I caught said, "Throw me back, Friend. I am
      a poet who walked on land, but traveled far

to get back to sea. My oxygen is air in water,
   my scales bright with longing to be less than man.
      A fish loves what he is, despising the rank smells

of rank, Rex's wrecks, fantasia's tatty oriflammes.
   See the banquet tables of stars plunge themselves
      back into the void, traveling in and out of lighted

parlors, pale with desire for the oxygen-filled sea?
   Leave the mess of well-beeved grandees blowing
      like grampuses, hurricanes slowing to local storms.

O fisherman, if you could but write like a fish,
   seeing branches of lightning vein the bouffant clouds,
      knowing that whatever we do will take painful,

beautiful, too constricting forms.—Can you hear
   Canopus buzzing beside your ear, casting his pilot's
      spell upon the water? See how dark swells swallow

and kill the great ship's lights? I must remain Lord
Landless, swimming in cold showers of moonlight
and specks of gold phosphor. *Throw me back*!"

FILM NOIR

Some girls, desiring experience,
uncover the beast who will not turn,
but stays pure butt-
ugly beast in an undifferentiated
dark bed of debauchery.

(Can you feel your belly warming?)

The beast eats innocence
which yearns for what—
bite-marks on the breasts, acid
pricklings of annihilation?
It takes a lot of blindness

to trust one's own seeing eyes,

to desire not
to be assaulted by unknown cries
and bites (Come in,
whoever, whatever. Do me, lick me,
break my legs, invade my womb).

—But what if a girl throws up

her hands, frantic to protect her own
sobbing baby from blows
and penetration of branches, bottles,
all things seen in the dawn as stupid,
ignorant, primitive,

and runs wild, looking for

a window, forces herself
to scream, forces herself
to vomit up the aphrodisiac
of despair, the dark beauty
of the word *dark*—the romance

of being killed?

ASTRONOMY

Virgin Hero
Teapot Doctor you are dots
to connect projections

of eyeballs fingers feet
to assure that everything
looks like me (I hear

a whippoorwill say its name
and a cardinal call sweetie
sweetie sweetie in its sleep)

Water Bearer Bull's Face
Cross I do not need you
You do not need me

now that I do not till
or sacrifice or look for signs
Heal Me Heal Me Heal Me!

ELEGY

All the males who fished these waters
are gone or going.

My brother is dying.
The nurses at dialysis have become his wives, sisters,
and daughters. He says they're his harem.
The doctor is his father, admired and faraway,
but bending to him now and then.

Who can love this old man now as he is?
Every day, flocks of ibis fly over him on Glass Island,
blowing like ribbons, changing leaders, the dark young
sometimes together, sometimes apart—

grains of dust gathering on their moving wings.

PIMPERNEL

In the rain, alizarin spatters & runs down towers.
The breasts of the whore weep with regret & compassion,
& the gates, all 28 of them, open & close,
clanking in the red tail lights.
                    Sirrah, then my face was my own,
all make-up washed away, nothing tweezed.
My eyes were wide-open catalpa blossoms
drinking rain, my mouth a green traffic light,
& men in tuxedos carried me arm over arm
from the Trocadero to the Stork Club.
            I had never heard of Darcy, so lately dead,
hit by a flower-pot thrown by a monkey,
but I caught his desire for me, red-handed.
            —Yet, in the long run, what could be better
than knowing one's own worth—
though by the time I recognized her, Truth,
                    pushing a shopping cart,
had hot-footed her sweet face & tattooed butt out of town.

POEM FOR JOE BOLTON

We saw the fever blister

                                        supernovas have no free will.

inside the corner of your mouth.

                                        Perhaps they have wanted to be

Saw you touching it, rolling it

                                        swallowed up in light for so long

with your tongue, waiting

                                        that they explode, scattering

for the incisor to bite down

                                        parachutes of glitter across the cold

hard, letting pus and blood

                                        black bayou between the worlds.

run out. Yet, perhaps

A QUIET WALK

All my life I wanted a mind flush
with reason, exact as the point
of a plumb-bob, but, hell, it's June

and tonight I want to love everybody

I mean really love them down to their
clammy feet, ridged and imprinted
by all the buckles, tongues and eyelets

of all the shoes they have to wear

and I want to help everybody escape
and feel their souls and bodies
flutter together and throb as one

Now I'm turning onto some avenue

crowded with fragrance, not like Johnny-
one-note roses, but cloudy with fresh
everything in bloom all at once

Overhead the cicadas are screaming

Alleluia, rubbing their heels or something
together on a loud rollercoaster of love
Though I took a solemn vow never

ever to put cicadas in any poem

here they come falling out of the dark trees
flinging themselves by the thousands
at my feet, coral pushpin eyes, filigreed

wings and moist little bodies flush with love.

WHY HUMPTY WENT SMASH

The day that Humpty went
Smash I was walking in the Tourmaline
Gardens when yellow splashed

My shoes and my face—
Shock waves from hell,
We were all yellow.

Sears, Detroit, estuaries,
Africa, Greenland, the whole world ran.
And only the faint surprise

Of your skin clinging to
My skin would not wash off before the
Great wind began to blow

All the duodecimo pages away
With the Annes, Janes, Elizabeths, Darcys,
Captain Wentworths, Bingleys, all

Those heroes and heroines
Who know the desperate reality of both
Soul and body. Was one kiss

So deadly shocking that
You are horrified forever? I tell you
That my soul was in love with

Your soul. Was Humpty going
Smash the cause of all the misery on this
Footstool earth—AIDS, crime,

Fathers turning away from
Mothers and both, like saints for hell, turning
Away from the children?

It did not begin in cheap starlight
Or crashing music, but perceived itself true
As *Persuasion*'s heroine. It was

Alma, that pure voluptuary who
Obfuscates everything. I have nothing more to say.
It was Alma. Turn the page.

2.

And then Finestra said,

"Why wouldn't I write about windows?

All my poems are about escape."

THE PILOT

Afterwards, I ran out of the flames,
past contrails, over the curve of the earth.
I have not eaten for months. No longer
want a roof over my head. I had wives,
some children. No matter. All lines
are parallel. I watch the farmer ride
his big yellow machine. Leaning over
the sill, I look into his eyes and whisper
Go Home. At night the moon's mouth
opens and moans *Go Home*. I lie beside him,
stroke his face. We kiss each other's
burnt lips. He whispers into my ear
Go Home. At the moment of bird, I fly.

SOMETHING ABOUT SPACE WHICH SADDENS

No horseshoe but a comet
hangs over my lintel.
Bending over the ears of corn,

space is a transparent bowl
flecked with froth and albumin,
but I have chosen this burrow,

rearranged its twigs and pebbles,
speak only to local zephyrs,
and saw away at my own violin.

I no longer look far ahead
at the violent colors surging
above the fields. I hardly

breathe, no longer wanting
to swarm through the eons,
looking to mate with God,

no longer buzzing around the light
which travels in folds like draperies.
All places are real places.

SHE STARES INTO SPACE

Sometimes a storm breaks through a window
and moves in, but things rarely happen here:

a shoebox eclipse now and then, various
Cavaliers and Puritans, vainglorious victims

and aggressors in dirt alleyways, heads stuffed
in dustbuckets, the fading sound of birdsong.

—But there, the vast loneliness of fledgling
planets, bitter-smelling rocks in empty rivers,

not decaying in patience like houses or bodies
slowly sinking—but firming, moons jockeying

like China juggled out of a cupboard, sills
of valleys leaning over, learning mold and lichen.

The loneliness of these child planets!—Their
gargantuan dusks, unthinking applegreen sunsets,

not one sparrow in a tree, not one martyr
or lover crying for a lost mate, brooded over,

brooding. Garnet-green pools engulf smaller pools
without quenching one thirst—yet all things

breathe in and out. Clouds pump their wings
and erupt into geysers, constellations sway,

collapse and smash like chandeliers. The debris
became fish, then mermaids, then girls—*then me.*

WASHING MY HAIR

Washing my hair,
leaning over
in the shower,
my head turned, dropped
into my hands,
and talked to me
sternly like some
Prussian uncle—
"You think this is
a skull full of
your own scabrous
words? There is no
away from this
hugging in the
cemetery.
When you are there
with me, held by
no bridge of no
neck, when sleep no
longer restores
and food does not
nourish, and the
spirit stands thin
and bare, not fat
and local, but
stretching to the
beginning and
the end, not just
yours—everyone's
continents, earth's
agates, bony,

mossy-haired rocks,
bees still crawling
over the slab
of honey that
was you: they are
looking for the
hand that used the
knife.—I say to
you that people
are escaping
every moment."

GOODBYE, MY BUCKO

O mon brave, mon fur piece,
mon hair shirt, mon bucko,
your lucky feet are crossing
the highway like a squirrel
ambling the arms of trees,
their leaves flying feathers

with veins, toward a hump
of clouds hiding, I've heard,
a golden camel—all our fret
but the weavings of insects
or a skirl of imaginary crows.
Add an N, a crow becomes

a crown. Are you scrambling
toward a castle in the creek
covered with leaves, about
to divine the diviner, red-handed?
Do you see me here, picking apples
by moonshine, a pony-ride away?

BLACKHEART, THE PRISON GUARD

I am dear old Blackheart, the prison guard.
I bring a plate of tamales to your youth,
And gild your golden lily with a crock of lard.

The drugs I sell are hope, next year, Corona
Beer and paying off the sacred plastic card.
A persistent innocence has enlarged this face,

This happy fishbowl face with its tiny castle—
And inside that castle, a tinier me who hisses
"Raca!" and creeps to a tiny desk to write

"Send balm!" Outside, the Interrogator paces,
Facing the two hostages I could never free—
Nor would they go if I had wit to free them:

"You haff not given solace only to ME,
And you vill admit your guilt, you lying slut."
I want to help her, grimace like a chimpanzee,

And roll back my lips in lying submission,
Lick his human-skin boots, order pizza and shakes.
I touch his arm: "I know that your obsessions

Are thrilling, shameless, even holy in a sense.
Can I placate you in any way—regression,
Rye, folly, melancholy? Keats' incandescence?

May I soothe frictions, subtle addictions?"
I simper into the eyes of Caesar Adolescent,
And flutter. He speaks to the woman: "I am

Not entirely artless. You were never innocent.
Could I ever forgive you for VOT I MYSELF DO?"
The eyes are pinpricks. The bricks run red

When the beatings begin. I make dilled stew
With just a hint of thyme. The vertical lines
Between the woman's eyes grow deeper, blue

Veins crawl her son's pale chicken breast.
Even the woman's eyes look raped and hollow,
Deep-bored. I bring her water, Methodist

Obscurantism and Marxist tralala. I know
It makes her happy. We are so deeply shallow.
I natter and pat her wrist. I fluff her pillow.

THREE THINGS

Callow dualists duel too hard
with too-sharp points, pointing out
winter or summer, war, peace,

man, woman, dead, alive,

as if there were no skewed axis
spewing ice and flowers, no Muse
spinning airs from her lyre and wool

from her light and dark goats.

Those shriekers never weary
of wallowing in the corruptions
of the incomplete, never weary of

swallows falling dead at their feet,

felled by scolding contrasts, scalding
bombasts.—Bemused, baffled,
Belinda pictures a priceless portrait

sliced into two worthless pieces,

and sets her mind steadily on three things—
a desert tortoise waiting years
under scorching sand for rain,

the flowerings of pain

and pleasure
in the face of the cellist, and the planet
patiently pulling rabbit ears of time

out of the black top hat of space.

THE WEDDING

I had no father to do it, so my hands
gave me away. Rhett, back from
the blockade, once searched them
& knew I was a field hand, damn him.
My bouffant frock sailed up the channel,
a schooner full of unlucky charms.

Joe took my hand, lifted my veil,
exposing me to alternate dimensions
leaking out, & bussed me. I don't
know why gravity is so unexplainably
weak. I don't know what love means,
though it was never exactly mean

to me—tongue stuck out, showed its
fanny, spat on my satin pumps
& such like. But what would you do
if you didn't have love? Raise your
hand back there, you in the tweeds
& the pipe. Say anything. It'll be wrong.

THAT ONE

Her with her jiggery pokery
& flamethrower pants of joy
        Her with her shameful nights
& talk of riding out storm waves
in an open pine-needle basket
        she wove herself
from its loud green fragrance
Her with her finger in her ear
        asymmetrical soul 2/3 in daylight
2/3 in outer darkness
hearing shadowy troops

        fumble tumble & blurt about her
scaring & almost
delighting her so that her book
        had hundreds of chapters
each one royally titled
Juvenalia Saturnalia Glossolalia
        straight out of Homer or somebody
dark-rosy-wine-fingered
& she told me to hold out
        this bog lily to you Take it
smell it touch it you'll love it

& to tell you that there is no
        earthly way to come to you
except by walking on water
to & from the gusty island kingdom
        booming with surf where two
vast eyes one eternal light
one eternal dark stare

out to sea where the swamp bubbles
an orgasmic blue flame doves roar
snapdragons pop & spit fire
& the fool moon rings like a gong.

A MEETING OF THE HISTORICAL SOCIETY

Fellow members of this vast family
surnamed Grief-taster have you noticed
all these hellos & not one goodbye

as ghosts collect fluttering under the dash
fishing for loose Life Savers the engine
sputtering droplets of potent life dripping

down the windshield hardening into frost
freeze & thaw dirty snow spinning
underneath the wheels & under that

the underground river heaving?
Greetings to everyone from everywhere
always leaving never returning circling

the globe like Puck like air however carsick
the cry of the beast bellowing in the wind
Go ahead & look at those crushed cars

gliding by stacked in trucks (Flexi-God
in his Flexi-World) You won't see Shakespeare's
car there—gone ahead no issue—even as

he keeps showing us there is nothing but
Duration Ah Friends the rest is bogeys bonging
our spines like xylophones or half-lit

Madame Mortmain tipping out a surly
stinking mannikin in grave clothes to waltz
Keep in mind—especially you Father—

the eternal war between first & last names—
tender once-&-for-all new & particular breath
versus the old novelette O always this same old

bitter quarrel between the real & the idea
of the real even as every mother's son of us
was conceived in some kind of ecstasy

in the radiance of the back seat
A good time was had by all or some
A show of hands please I thought so

Next month bring secrets buzzing
under Auntie's lap robe & O yes
some favorite ejaculation of your

grandfather to share My Grampa Fred
used to mutter *By Jol* under his breath
Thank you for your kind attention.

Let's join Ida Hoare-Cox & Marion Pugh-Wee,
waving their hankies at us from the picnic table.

II

FATHER ALONG SAYS GRACE

Each of us in this numerous family surnamed Grief-tasters,
attracted as we are to treetops, gongs, photos of galaxies,
St. Stephen's shining face as he is being stoned by a crowd
happy to be outraged, so that they can do
what they wanted to do anyway,

We who fly high on the wings
                    of economy & moderation into a googol
of saints naked in top hats, caps, capes, fright wigs,
prison stripes, riding above the drooling madhouse,
            above the storm humming & chittering like bats,
We who weary of the rigors of plot
                    as our souls weary of the ordeals of the body
& love anything we can count unaccountable,
            For us Death's breath coming near we find so
unaccountably sweet that it cures us permanently
of all that ails us & breaks the ball-peen hammer
                    of our hearts' old sorrow. Amen.

While Pat scribbles a love song called THESE ALTERNATE UNIVERSES ARE HONEY DRIPPING THROUGH BREAD

The world flowing hot & cold
I cannot keep (even) you from scalding
or freezing or wind from blowing through
our empty skulls even now tumbling apart

Now is the keep of our sheepfold, romance
of glance & knee the bed on which
we used to leap, our baby beamed upon
beaming her feet gums tiny fists beating

the air as you & I now beam at our newest
baby the starry sky a saxophone of moon
turning the silver night gold, the sun stuck
on empty (your beautiful mouth) our life on go.

THE ESCAPE ARTIST

& then It said to itself
let's stick it to her about the sorrow of animals
& how people practice on them to learn mercy
& invade her with how security is just
another illusion like the toothpick castles

called Church & Family & penetrate her
with being used for lust when she in earlier
days would have murdered or murdered herself
in rage & shame & convict her with the innocent
suffering she herself unleashes & the hard work

of building further illusions of security
& how the children who issue from her body
must be taught to murder just enough to regret it
& not go too far & now that she has not one stay
in old age & its hope (for hope in a future

is happiness) she sees the futile wheel turn
how little but something changes—& though
It never left her she thought about it less & less
& noticed (har) that it looked like a wad of mesh
torn mesh & told herself that she could probably

squeeze herself through an opening while It said
nothing but licked its chapped chops & held out
its arms to her, supple suppliant, & fondled her
backside whimpering but seeing she was lost to It
It turned quickly to another also busy folding herself

through one of the wire windows bound then loose
    & she saw how nothing but her bias toward
the good & the verities of children & how it was
    better to recognize beauty than be beauty
to love the oil-slick rainbow torn in a ditch rather

    than be the rainbow lying in a ditch (grim
knowledge being better than beautiful ignorance)
    had escorted her into the arms of the good conductor
now taking her elbow & hurrying her up the staircase
                                        into the bright open.

SHE MEDITATES ON FLOWERS

They do not will themselves to drop,
or saw themselves off the bough
with knives, but appear and disappear
on time, cold and heat their bits

and bridles, renewable as swans.
They bear torn chemises in sickening
purples without vanity, dozing
under a silver lantern until the hot,

golden one arises. They lead invasions
of spiders and bees through commonplace
pinks or yellows straight to the intimate,
moist, sweet spot, so that tall, bronze-

helmeted armies refill the fields.
She understands: *If I fix on one*
or a few blossoms, I am bound for sorrow.
If I love them all, indiscriminate as God,

I am bound to be patient and happy,
and achieve satori at least by old age.
Yet, among the tranquil flocks, submitting
their seeds so easily to time and fate,

she admits to a certain defect in temper.
I will never forget you, my own few blossoms,
no matter how many crowd forward to take
your place, drowning the earth in coarse,

cold-blooded perfumes. And that is why
the world depends on me, the Holy-in-Battle.
A sword flashed—she became enlightened,
gave up poetry—then snatched it back again.

MUSIC FROM THE CAVE

A small-boned Belgian girl heard
the far-off singing of troglodytes
in caves where water drips in basins,
and mapped their dark itineraries
in the deep rocks beneath her feet—

Mlle Arbre, she planted a willow tree
in a Windsor garden turning endlessly
under moons by day and night, small
rains and meteor showers, the windy
flickerings of Aldebaran, Altair, Pisces—

Cancer put out each bit of light
in cell and bone. When old manor bells
mutter, shivering in breezes at night,
and begin to roll, long, low, melodious—
veiled hopes begin to breathe and stir

among crystal stalagmites, ruffling
pools where blind fish sleep, and then—
pantalooned houri, she dances,
while her husband holds his breath
and storms the seraglio of his dreams.

IN THE AUDIENCE

One of the poets was hitting few notes,
but they were strong. The other flew
too much with angels. And you are somewhere

in the audience, your eyes oddly hooded,
probably vowing never to use loons,
looping, or ferns in your poems, especially

potted ones. You who look so beautiful
or so drained, variable as the sun covering
and uncovering with clouds, mud flats

and tide in flood, I feel your presence
like a kind of mating, one spotlight
shining in two places. This air is charged

with fidelities and infidelities of spirit,
hiding our multiple, deliberate amputations,
for we are children of the past, easily

awed and easily aroused. Now I taste
the varicolors of your flame. Even that
red light blinking *Danger Danger* must see us

burning away in the night air and know
—it is the unconsummated inner life
of dying things that makes them glow.

AT THE MOVIES

1

I'm at the Ritz so I can eat popcorn from the floor and get redemption, Nonpareils, God, there's Don necking up a storm with you-know-who. All hands on deck back there! Sad but true, here in Florida, satyrs like nymphs, and nymphs sure as hell like satyrs. Look at Marilyn turn around, craning her ugly neck for Mr. Wright, the sponsor of Future Teachers from the Canadian Shield, fearful handsome and backward. I like the movies because everything looks like it should—clothes, faces, houses. Last night on the History Channel I saw an interview with a terrorist—soft pink face, soft pink shirt. Wardrobe, casting—wrong, wrong, wrong. I never know what to think when I've left the Ritz. You know where you are with movies. Roses smell better in black and white.

2

There are many paths into a lovely face (think Joan Fontaine, Linda Darnell, Vivien Leigh), but only one way out of a strong one (think Bette Davis, Joan Crawford, Agnes Moorehead). Connected to music and the open face of the moon, a beautiful face binds one forever and places one's feet on a road to beauty where things can go many ways, because many things are true. A strong face says, *Life is hard. You'll never be strong enough, good enough. Your tires end up shredded, whether you back out or go ahead.* A beautiful face, receptive as sand or water, whispers, *Look, Sweetheart, we escape with or without the body.*

3.

Jesus over the altar winks at me:

“Sure I’m wonderful,

but don’t let it ruin your life.”

RUSHING HEAVEN

I used to be a vestal virgin, crude
and disgusting, who consulted Magister Bluejay
or crawled through the trees at 3 a.m. to buy
the crone's healing cherries, while she pumped
bellows of praise to the god of Wind, Hurikan.

But when the blood poured over me like wind
when sun drops into the lake, I gave up fake
enchantments, bog sprites, cobwebs and ructions.
Dangling on sharp horns, I plunged into the noble
Dark Ages, and fell into God before he thought

of dividing up, back when he rolled his tongue
around himself like a marble or sheep's eye,
before he raised a window in himself and looked out
(those who have legs, let them come if called; add
another A, a place becomes a palace), back before

he expanded from a trickle in the middle of the hill
into spring, waterfall, sprung rhythm, river, time,
space, and so on, before he discovered his left
and right hands, invented rhetoric or fell in love,
or thought up the elements, or made corpses' eyelids

flutter, or used the alias, Lord Destruction, to lay
the axe to every trunk, or tumbled like a dead man
into church and politics—and now I sit down inside
him and pull the doors and windows shut, and ask for
nothing but to be alone with him and watch the fire.

BURIED STATUE

I recognize those nails,
the coarse thin hair

which runs delicious
through me when I touch it—

the right side of the lips
more strangely sensitive

than the left. Vines
of sand slip shivering

down my body. A small river
trots nearby—the Tigris?

This could be Ur or Tyre.
In a thousand years of

tonguing clay, we may be
discovered—a cozy field

of statues running unbound.
The imagination swells

empty, a balloon over my head—
bag of wind whose reflux

might taste of sulfur water
and lightning, but only makes

milk like an udder to
feed something something—

and to sense the whereabouts
of that enormous colossus

struggling his way toward us
through the gravel pit of stars.

MIDNIGHT SORTIE

He walks with no lantern, knocks at a door—
then runs.
When he dozes on broken slabs
in the graveyard, bullfrogs are his watchdogs.
A platoon of pines fills up
with yellow-crowned night herons.
—And this is where we who breathe
haunted furniture owned by idols
quail under cover,
wandering deeper into our eiderdowns, mumbling,
Who is the one who laps my pain,
loves its ebb and flow—
Eats me by his presence?
Feeds me by his absence?
When he falls asleep, electric storms
strip knowledge from my bones
and my children curse me,
but I dream of woodpeckers
hammering nests in dead trees, chips flying.
Satisfied, he regards me from half a moon's face.
And when my vicious pride
clots, shakes loose, and clatters out
like a marble thorn,
my adolescent soul surges and reverts
into its inevitable and singular shape—
as I roll in the odors
of long grasses and wild lilies,
head swimming
in iliads
of invading green moonlight.

WALKING WITH YOU IN ASPEN

Not even in love with God,
but with your own pure,
fastidious soul,

like God, you come and go—
mostly go. And write
great letters,

like Rilke. You may be
just another Faust
setting up Marguerite

to strangle your child.
Old luxury, spirit
without flesh,

loving you is like
having sex with angels.
They sip souls.

I cannot breathe up here.
Now you climb—I wait
under black trees

for light. Venus is rising.
Trees crash high
in a mountain avalanche—

You are the tree who slides
down the scree, green
and tall, to a lower place.

I thought you might like
    these clean pavements—
        the modulated voices

of the rich, their surprised eyes,
    tiny zucchinis and patty
        pan squashes in their net

shopping bags—but when your
    fingers intertwine with mine,
        Venus goes down,

Scorpio comes up—and your
    heart is in the castle,
        the transcendent tree,

the Princess—beyond the pond
    of fire straddling this galaxy.
        Beyond all human help.

COLD POEM

This is a cold poem, written
at the back of a cave where
many people died. Their
eyes cruise like alligator eyes
in the dark. Don't touch
this poem. It wouldn't like it.
Go to the beach. Go to a movie.
Shop for the doodads you love.
My God kills before he cures,
then kills again. He suits me
down to the ground. Your fingers
are beginning to stick to the
page. Under no circumstances
touch your tongue to this poem.
Do not try to eat this poem.
It is full of germs. It gives
a deadly case of flu. Take
vitamins. Put on a coat. Get
out of here while you have
time, before you get the shakes.
Too late. *I warned you, sucker.*

THE MOTHERS

This city is such a lovely
grave, where spirits walk
in the cool of an evening
(no man has life enough

to build a life in you—those
butterflies are not lovers
winding around each other,
but around the column of air

between them), so here we are
in the grassy park, assigned
to the comfort and dignity
of dogs, lights of the world,

constructs of safety, turning
twigs into wands and rocks
into bowls of water—
where mothers smile at each other's

gains and losses, pushing swings,
waiting at the ends of slides
for children who already smell
the sweet perfume of something

dead, their eyes already old,
suspicious, panting to sniff out
where the men have gone—
Someplace Else, Anybody Else

playing in them like auroras,
lifting golden beakers
of pathogens to their lips,
opening like lids on caskets

of secret, forbidden jewels—
the moon's pearly, pock-marked behind
beaming through faery, burglar-
proof sashes onto fresh faces.

WARNING FOR A DAUGHTER

Do you understand?
The universe is a cheap, wind-up whizzy

toy, a duck that walks, if you are not
with me. The father cannot be happy
without the son, and that is the whole
of religion. You made me Mother,

and now I am your own insatiable
child, who first were mine. How not

to inflict this presence on you, this
terrible heat running hot orange,
bubbling, eddying, carrying boulders
and logs, spurting unexpected jets

all over your mountain, spewing stones,
tossing volcanic rock for miles,

spoiling your careless meadow
where time lies cool and hazy,
as I hear my footsteps receding
on the bridge. Even now I am

reaching rivers of fire
toward you, above the timberline

where your pockets of snow stretch
white in the sun. See, even the clouds
are rolling toward you. *Run for your*
life, I say, run for your life.

MESSAGE FROM SPACE

We do not know you.
Apology. Big ones remember
the space between us.
We are abundant,
speak from the sands
of our feet. Our sign
is The Boy singed
but walking. We see you
in evening air when rain
fools the discs, this
and that, nearby, farthest.
Same sweet nothing for you?
Do you edible good words
in your cheeks?
Do you righteous
or moving color?

CHAMELEON

I will not talk
about the horrors of making
love, casting and absorbing
these infinite shades which
jangle like ropes of ankle bells.

In all this time I have tried
to become one thing at a time.
Upon the blue table I am blue,
on green, green. My tail falling
over an edge becomes the color

of air and flies. My head, peering
into the closet full of ants,
is dark-lobed, jewel-encrusted
with cabochons, Grand Vizier
of Oceanic Confines, the tail

still flecked with pantry light,
a leopard of high spring. Here
in your heart reading, I am
a splinter of red. Looking with
your farsighted, hazel eyes,

I grow pale. You, my Bedouin,
are too many. As I approach
the end, staring into the garnet sun,
I see that each color has been
a prison to me. You will see

me shrunken black, a narrow leaf
in the carpet, but I will be
free from the tents of one word—
splashing like a wild camel
in the nile green of none of them.

MOVIE WITH A DEAD POET

I went to see "L'Atalante."
   Embarrassing—good in the telling
      but not in the watching. How

can lovers ever find each other
   before FIN and the lights come on?
      89 minutes isn't very long. He asked

if he could sit beside me, fresh
   from prison. He liked the peeling paint
      and the dirty curtain. He even found

pathos in the old New Yorkers there
   on a Monday afternoon. He was crazy
      about the popcorn. I whispered,

"I love your poems." He told me
   about prison, that it's like some
      obvious, boring movie directed

by someone too stupid to approve
   of happy endings, endlessly screaming
      "Happiness is immoral, you *muzhiks*!"

I asked him why suffering gives
   simplicity and strength that crack
      the rocks of an age. He said,

"I don't know." And then, "Honest to God,
   it's a good movie and all that,
      but I can't stand my heart to be

broken one more time. I'm scared
    to death he'll drown or she'll get
        run over or forced to a life of shame.

TOO LATE terrifies me. The only thing
    I can stand now is happiness and that
        isn't art." We'd have walked out,

but the hero and heroine were kissing.
    "Thank God that's over," he cried,
        and disappeared into sunshine.

TERMS

Just as "clouds and rain" was used by the ancient
Chinese as a delicate euphemism for love-making,
so Proust employed the cattleya orchid as a verb for
copulation. Similarly, instead of "having sex," we might
substitute something about a rainstorm—or, since French is
always attractive for the purpose, "tremblements de terre."
The whole private region might be called "les jongles,"
the "delicatessimus" or the "delicatessima." Artists could
begin to call pubic hair "furze," "fern," "gorse," or "heather."
To express the traditional hope and essential nobility of the
male member we might arrive at terms such as "oakensii
mysterium," "rivendell," the mighty "prix," "startler,"
"herculaneum," etc. We could call a woman's secret parts
the "dahlia," "plumeria," "phloxen," or, more scientifically,
for the general area, the "camellia japonica" (definitely
"clematis," instead of that other word). Her swaying breasts
might be called "les danseurs," "les soeurs," "les globes
mystiques," "les hirondelles," even "the swimmers."
A gynecologist would be a "lagoonist," a urologist a
"deliquescent fluxist." Like the natural world, or matter
itself, what are words but the radiant energy to whirl in
and out of forms? And what are science and spirit but
outer lobes and fiery recesses of the same voluptuous
beauty lying in our arms? As we ruffle her lobelia,
she gathers us into her gloriosa.

THREE A.M.

for Blema

Curtains move above the lake
like some brooding king
taking a walk
in his nightgown.
As waves of electrons
flow from the sun,
our own electrons blow
like curtains opening and closing.
Such tender brevity,
these flickering folds—
our own tiny neon nightgowns
still sparking fancies
out of natural,
actual fire.

AFTER THE SWAN

"Wrath of Perfume,
I have certain generative responsibilities.
It takes a deuce of desire to make a world.
Do you think I like to swan around,
making silly girls into slugs and ladybugs?
If you knew
how hard it was to beat those wings—I'm not
a young man, after all—to overtake
and mount that flailing mass of feathers, snaky
necks entangling like fishing lines. Not exactly
good for the heart—
and half the pleasure, so pitifully fleeting, comes
from knowing you, you minx, are watching (admit it,
you always are). And then of course,
I have to advance their issue.
Women
can be so frighteningly violent about their children."
He stood. "I feel surf stinging
pearly iridescent thighs east of Macedonia.
Fresh flesh.
That's all they understand down there. And you,
Mistress Complaint, do you ever ponder
why I keep you?"
After the thunderclap of his passing,
she shouted, "You'd think such a powerful old goat
might wield some power over the state
of his loins.
Make delirious virgins careen
over my head, spangle the sky, leer, spin
and spawn at my feet.
I am Hera,
honored by my dishonorable lord,

for I do keep him, though not faithful.
I too am creation's royal brat,
whose duty flies beyond law
into unspeakable freedom."

Watching a hump of island appear and disappear
in the waves, she thought she saw the back of her
fast-swimming husband—
or was it a stag,
his antlers high as a tree, pushing the water
—and then everything around her,
the peacock roosting on a branch, his tail
cascading, swaying like an old man's beard,
the heifer snorting in the pasture,
the old gold of the tulip tree—
all the earth was pouring out
pieces of him.
She heard a baritone rumble in her ear,
"Hera is the cold opal
containing a fleck of my fire,
a finished work—
not wet pigment
running down the paper, a full-blown peony,
not pollen on the wind searching for a pistil,
a tall pine, not the pinecone falling,
spilling its seed."
Over her, the peacock stood,
spreading his thousand-eyed tail,
shaking out a flurry of rods, cones, rakes, bones,
flukes of irises, ruptured snakes, viruses,
flakes of bitter, dark, torn things—

a slurry of glitter lit up by the sun.

LUNCHEON AT THE CLUB

See the women taste peppermint ice cream
with heavily plated restaurant spoons, almost
  finished with husbands and children.

See the men drink bourbon in the clubroom,
finished with sorrow, looking toward oblivion.
  See how the blankness of the sky comes on,

how it apes blue and black, but never spoils.
See people stacked underneath like brushwood—
  under the sun, uniform piles of gold nuggets,

under the moon, cartons of mushrooms to be sold.
Now sex is indistinguishable—the men are dead
  spirits looking down at their women looking up,

each of them thinking of gold and the stock market,
and how nice a little creme caramel would taste,
  thinking how time ate up everything and moved on,

thinking how fast and how far they had been pulled
out of the forest over the tundra to the straits,
  into this impossible, unfamiliar world.

A SIMPLE REQUEST

for Wes

Here I am, still drowning in the world,
while you are opening Dame Simplicity's closet—

and I say, Be good to him, Simple Goodness,
Air and water, expand for him! Moon, be a smiling
china plate for him to leap over!

In the cupboard where cups wait quietly
and beautiful old words are folded in flannel cloths:

Mother, Father, Longsuffering, Beloved, Forgiveness—

Lay him down in simple peace, homely pleasures,
between jars filled with feathers and shells—
near Grandmother's broom that sweeps so clean.

What aromatic, wild poultice crushed to the breast
soothes and heals all?—

It is the essence of Brother
overpowering me with some stinging nettle of sweetness—

Whatever sunset door you go through, hold open for me.

THE SEAMSTRESS

When the boat arrived,
I stepped over the gunnel,
my flannel skirt stiff with rime.
The horrible blankness
over the lake remained—
no mountains or trees, just
an intermittent chalk-line
with nothing above it, until one
tree rose above the monotone.
Hours later, we docked at a pier.
That one tree—now huge—

was tumbling with globes
of dew, all colors running here
and there, so that I thought
death was not so bad.
Left on shore, the other
passenger and I sat under
the tree, warming ourselves
in our own reflections,
hearing the tree whisper,
Where was our sun born?
How did it get here?

See my still-dark hair
in a weedy snood, his
hazel eyes and pallid hands?
We lie under the tree, adding
our own small vividness,
our colors absorbing into
its colors. Sometimes I sit up

and wave at you over there
in the sheeny dawn, vacant
as the glare of old linen
and rotten silk.

SECRET LOVERS

Drifting noonish, our faces politely
turn toward admirers, perspiring.
Clouds mass, lights turn on the valley,
tinkling ankle bells, while we shift
and adjust, separate, entwined, aware

only of each other, a cool flush of color
in our cheeks. I turn away, inflamed,
pretending not to know how easily
the currents of withholding and sending
transmit fire along my lightning's path.

—Here, half in, half out, floating
in a skiff issued by the palace, reflecting
how prepositions determine destiny,
how the word *air* is nothing but air,
how pleasant the words *sunup* and *flybys*,

we look through each other, crying out
at a volley, a flourish, a fumarole,
a mist of tree-colored birds lifting
effortlessly out of the flues of the chimneys
of the roofs of the impenetrable forest,

hovering, their beaks skimming the water—
the inexorable fanning of their wings
blowing our faces, our clothes, our
habillements of secrecy, into a new reality
we created and called out of its nest—

racing low over the river toward us.

TREE, RIVER, CLOUD

Under a cottonwood tree
so old, so vast
that yellow leaves drift down like snow,
our bare feet dance,
caressing the tree's roots,
encouraging it to live.
Under the tree
a river,
the great snake,
coils and bends,
carrying my heartbeat, your lifeblood,
lightning in its tail,
two living leaves in its mouth.
At night the river wakes,
rises and walks,
becomes Cloud Serpent,
its brilliant shadow flying over us,
rustling, shaking out gold feathers
like leaves,
encouraging us to live.

TURNBACK

Something old has ended Turn
back the pages of the bigfat
Unabridged far from Psychotic
to before History back to Apple

or better yet the Preface with
its birdlike numerals iv, v, vi,
and vii We need no sage to tell
us where to turn Our future

spreads before us like a patient
etherized upon a table about
to wake up after a long almost
successful operation the tumor

sucked out of the brain the heart
unblocked hips and knees replaced
cataracts gone arteries scraped
clean tubes tied hammertoes and

hemorrhoids corrected a cage
of infection excised—and here
we are arrived at A what scope
how time spreads before us

like a trip around a bigger sun
Nothing ahead but everything
to free us from the rage of custom
the snarl of dogma the vogue

of exigence scared into rebellion
and back again—and all those unborn
poets set to blast us out of here
wherever that is O one more time.

4.

Let us assume that it is good to be
mortal, not to have enough time
or strength to amount to much,
that we are buried in an earth
that needs our blood and accepts her
stillborn child as alive in her heart.
Let us assume that it was worthwhile,
that light sparked by friction,
however soon it went out.
And let us assume that the work which ate us up
deepened into something good for the earth,
that it was not the wheel turning
inexorably, but a wheel traveling
to a private dawn, throwing off sparks.

CLOUD STUDY

We were hurrying to the train.
Clouds walked briskly overhead
in grey or amber lace.
We knew there would be a war,
that we were made of grass.
We were holding hands, of course.
Who knew if we would marry?
All things are veiled,
covering the life within.
Our own sun, now covered,
blotted out other suns sprawling around us.
But my own tiny diamond,
too close a star to be easily eclipsed,
sparkled openly.
As we arrived in town,
clouds were walking faster, dressed
for dinner in feathers and opals.
Nature was pushing us to get on with it,
and we did, always obeying Mother
in spite of ourselves.
When the downpour came,
we slipped into the King's Arms,
and shook ourselves awake, like dogs
spraying raindrops
into separate, primary colors.
Clouds in white nightgowns
stood around, watching us
fall asleep.
The night awoke to flak
and cracked like a whip.
We ran into clouds,
dressed in black ribbons.

NAKED WOMAN

Truth is a naked woman
slipping through the gate, the elms,
the sullen apartment buildings,
as if she wanted me to follow,
but not see clearly or too much.
It's the slipping away
that makes her Truth,
the not marrying me
and sitting calmly on my terrace,
for all the world to see.
It's making me discontented
with what I have, and opening up
the world, wider,
more unattainable,
sorrowful and smoky pink
with cleavage—
that mystical cleavage,
half-lit shadows shuddering
between pillowy headrests
and billowy settees. See how
she looks at me from that hillock,
hand on hip (the tart), calling,
Catch me if you can, Big Boy.

TO HIM AND HIM

Passionate, austere
Puritan word-circus, pit
of glory, tell me
what you see now,
cloudy-driven man of action,
one-man band playing
oboe, drum and cornet.
It was that damned jar
and the funny guitar
conjoined with hard winter's ice
and summer auroras
that made our green and purpling
spires spring taller.
You entered as a lover
disguised by a Cymbidium orchid
in your lapel, seduced, but not fatally,
by beauty, and left as a lover
waiting in a familiar room,
its windows wide open.
You spun so fast, plump
brown fox, that your dark velvet fur
caught our own dark sparks
with effulgences of fire.

DEAD AMERICAN BOY

The ceiling is mottled
with mountain ranges like Mars'.
The eyes of the boy
turn inward, worshiping
the fire roaring out of the broken cells.
His pulse has gone AWOL, flown over the mountains
to an island they say cannot be found
by boat or air. The island,
part of the chain called Inconceivable,
sits in the Gulf like a stone in the throat,
round as a black band on the arm,
puckered as mountain ranges.
His mother, hair flying, wild Magellan,
is on her way by air and boat. She knows
that, though continents sink,
her boat will sail, and a new island must rise, must rise
with her dead boy on its back.

Gather round me as grackles call
under a sky mackerel with a touch of shrimp
as psychics fall through holes in clouds
& dinky wisdom fairies fall dead at our feet
Come close to my lawn skirts all twisted strings
of DNA up & down quarks & heavier
strange quarks that form at a higher density

all 2-& 4-chambered hearts you you & even you
For I Queen Reality in day-glo green tell you
as lightning precedes thunder as magnets draw
metal filings the Worthies are gathering higher
& more valiant than that hussy Miz History
stumbling like a mummy unwrapping rotten gauze
dropping lips toes fingers nose Yes even now

as a new dragon & his dam shake off sleep
& the fingernails of human certainty sharpen &
squirrels chuk-chuk their ancient inscrutable anger
these Worthies gather to say Remember
hornbeam forests The roundness of live music
The lovely hatcheck girl Fedoras Auroras Polecats Pole
Stars Wisteria filling dead trees How weeping

is a sign of life in babies How a dead man feels no
chigger bites How we form from collapsing families
as stars form from the collapse of stars &
Just look at those half-moons rising in your fingernails
That's how the great ones talk my dears You know
how time flies from right to left across the earth
as weather flies from left to right how a little liquid water

mixes with a little geothermal heat & lo life flows
under the door like an attack of gas? Of course
you do Nestlings but most of all don't forget what
Mother cannot explain The delicious sun that shines
& does not burn but drips like rain
through our frail rafts wrestling a loud running sea
rushing to break on what shores?

SOLSTICE

Her life flowed out into her things.
The whole world danced upon her pulse.
Forests surged inside the electricity
of her marrow, sheltering other lives,
from pregnant mice to antique birds

who never walked upon the ground.
But as her life drew back, staring
at the museum of her past, an otter
tripped into a hole left by the taproot
of a falling pine, eggs refused to open,

butterflies morphed into caterpillars,
deer leapt into hunters' arms.
—Yet when the sun stepped back to take
another look, slipping through birds
sleeping on the lake, they burst

into the air, flapping thunderous wings.
Giant tree ferns unfurled, juniper
berries swelled fat, bobcats began
to lick each other all over. A pair
of buzzards mate in a hollow log,

rare and common moths coat
the crotches of trees, fish climb ladders.
The flamingo preens herself a louder
pink, swans are running on tiptoe.
The woman lifts her head, reforested,

sees herself as a migrating bird
of the same flock, pulled to the edge
and back by startling leaps, metes
and bounds, fed by an imperative of sun
in the blood, and breathes her

life back in—fiery, fecund, dangerous.

THE TURNING

I

You say that naturalness is as unnatural
as planting hair.

You say that I cannot be reproduced
by rhyme or night sweats.

You imply that Hotel Politico disembodies

to a zinnia, head and torso bathed in water
rancid with its own greenness—

the self so disembodied
that it can no longer be self-conscious—

an entity deprived of anything
but inner shedding, sloughing.

Can you feel it
loosen the primitive gesture?
—Feet, keep on moving.

II

You must admit that my argument
lightens the zinnia's sophistry

just as a wedding gown surrenders
to shore, subsumed

to seaweed, a haven of naked girls, mermaids

(predators eroticizing
the moon, meat crawling the shore).

You hear me
embodied in your own eyes

lashed to the mast,
my body dazzling the sapphire air—

but the sloop wades deeper,
beyond the old decolleté, beyond islands
into sea lanes.

Father no longer analyzes the Bounding Main

(its stupid sea survivors
empty pointless adventures
grotesque tyrannies sloshing, chattering
teeth in the foaming brine).

Heathen brutes lapped up all his strength.
Waves ground him into sand.
His toenails turned to jingle shells.

III

A transformer blew
shoptalk about Nietzsche, stormy petrel,
Lord of Windy Latitudes,
desert water-bird.

Leg irons and toe rings bathe his torso
in a pool of sea-green light.

That old river sank deep into American sand.
Where will it reappear?

You intimate that marbled flesh majestically
washed out of whoever's womb of light onto land
into heather, bog-and-bird logic.

But I hear incensed ravens shriek,
tearing out the belly of the sun: *It's you.*
It always was you.

IV

The breeding nest of everything, past,
present, science, the real,

including the atmospheric hooey
which amasses around it,

is being pressed down hard into a ball
and I fling it

whizzing into the future with small thought
of Art, that whorehound puzzling
between the smells of order and disorder

—nor is it aimed to fall
on the Continent Of Beauty,
that ornamental Hun, blubbering seducer

plummily intoning
into a champagne flute lit by glow-worms, his
heart a fist
of mortadella

(O mon bureaucrat, dripping all that ooh-la-la)

This time I turn
and aim it to land at the pediments

of another continent where the face
of a lighthouse
pierces stone windows and rotates its burden

of stinging light—
even as the sea eternally clears

its throat and dashes

heads, pieces and stems
of drowned zinnias against uncut rock.

SWIMMING IN PRELAPSARIA

I laze over the rills, the drone,
into green pools
edged by crows
crowing hard caws,
and into shallows,
scraping shins and ankles—
Where can Mother be? And Father, gone so long?—
to wider shores, maples on either side,
billowing like forest fires.
My feet won't touch, my arms are tired—
and both shores invisible,
lost in smoke.
The sound of my breathing, and fear
of some graygreen mossy arm underneath,
a suckered tentacle, reaching,
the sky falling like a banquet table,
the brush of something on my hip
rowing the water into curls,
the water like clay, my hands clay,
the shelf under my feet clay.
A step upward into cold air,
stumbling to another shelf—
I am born
into a bosque of willows.
Take my hand. Help me up.
We must build a house. *I must write this down.*

THE WOODCHUCK'S SONG

On this grade-A gray day the clouds
   a herd of bison stampeding over my head,
      the slag-colored lake all pizzicato,

a day when shades of drowned sailors
   cling together like beach-grass to wring
      their hands & moan, What Now What Now,

I shout Huzzah my Hearty to you, Reader,
   just as I salute the tenderest hartebeest
      thundering from a herd of galloping hyenas.

—Yesterday, peering through columns
   of hairy roots in my crabbed solitary lookout,
      considering the connection between Ravel

& travel, while svelte buzzards idly twirled
   over rafts of dead alewives washing onto shore,
      I saw a woman on the beach pick up

a plastic bag, jerk it angrily over her head
   & twist a rope of pearls around her neck
      to shut off all the air—but suddenly

a motorcycle drove past fast looking for her
   or the end of the road, & Reader, I found that
      I forgave again your flaccid faces, pendulous

lips, floating bellies, weasel eyes vibrating
   in the sun—remembered anew that you too
      are creatures of the Diaspora & recollected your

lightning turns from the lion's broiling breath—
all the work you plan & still must undertake
to escape the razored paws & red-hot gullet.

THE LAST GIANT

for Elling

See how these whoreson lordlings
strap me to their anvil cloud,
throw dynamite and fire ants

in my wounds, laugh and call it
balm? See how red badges flit
among steel-tipped pine needles?

—A red-winged blackbird, seduced,
deluded into a horde
of grackles. See how her prize,

a mistletoe berry, round,
liquid, glowing as a See
of earth, falls from quarrelsome

beaks and rolls into the dark?
Doomed forests fall with me—all
slanted pillars of moon, ferns,

gophers, peacocks—their beauty
blown away like flocks of birds.
If beauty could save the world,

I would have saved it. And yet
I became termite, snakebite,
sinkhole—and the monstrous wave

that flushes you out to sea.
Little squalls and petty snits,
small furors of small Führers,

as you extinguish me, your
own blank lives wink out like gnats'.
—But see how the secret words—

a blinding sun, the last kiss,
lost mother, beloved man—
stay gold in the keep of my

huge, swollen heart? And see this
torch that was my eye still try
to flash into the passes

of Feed-the-Fire Mountain, Sword
Gallery, Vermilion Wall
and Stone Mirrors—watching for

feathered men and the jade face
—that is to say, perfect men,
and the Heap of Purple Gold

that unites the worlds. Decide
for yourselves if my soul climbs
fragrant as temple candles,

or dribbles a rosy drool
down my chin. Fools, what you love
will be torn from you, gasping,

left as bait for the powers
of darkness to desecrate.
I leave you here, carrion.

NAUTILUS TO MOON

Today I felt a shock
deep down where lava feeds the sand
its bright eruptions—and then
I heard the wind say,
"Sailor, I blow
through hearts of oak and hearts of bronze,
but my home lies here in bells
of warm and cooling water."
Tonight, wind and water turn to lamps
that make me know no difference
between the fires of hell
and living flames of love.
—Gray-Eye,
I cannot believe your mantle commands
your form, pattern, and colors in cloudy precision.
I do not think you rise and fall
by my pneumatics of oil and gas,
nor could one bubble of trapped air
send you flying half a sun away
to catch on a wavering hook of stars.
Yet, the way you pull me into your white face,
I know you remember
how we rang together like silver gongs
when a wave of woven purple shells
floated a maze
between us close to dawn.

YOUR HOROSCOPE TODAY

Because the sun is in your house,
today will be verdant as the taste
of arugula. Do not taste
of the farkleberry or the glair
of an egg. Eschew tobacco.
Virgo the Undervalued, plant myrtle
around cemeteries, lilacs around
privies. Keep sweeping up fallen
flowers at Heaven's Gate.
You, Leo, in the zoot suit, get over it—
she's a Portia, not a Porsche.
Go deeper. The earth's core is
just as hot as the sun's surface.
(A private word to Madam Babe:
Nip it. Beware the uber-doofus.)
Don't whine, Libra.
You could be one of the poor lovers
on moonless Mercury or Venus.
Be thankful that yonder moon
licks you nightly with its silver tongue.
Yo, Cancer, get lost.
Pisces, that piece of salmon
last night was bad.
Sagittarius, gallop farther afield
to chomp the tender grasses.
Avoid horseshoe bats.
Scorpio, cool the sex appeal. Breathless
means not only excited, but dead.
Avoid lava lamps.
You depressives (ram, goat, fish and scales,
virgin, horseflesh, etc.), blue sapphires
of the Kosmos, listen to that voice

in the mirror unless it says *Slit*
Your Wrists. Of course you wasted
your life—what else was it for?
Snow White deepens into Rose Red,
just as constellations tumble down
the gullet of the western sky.
Avoid blood oranges.

Taurus, give up fixed convictions.
Eroticism's bigger than that.
Capricorn, ix-nay on the goatee.
Avoid tin cans.
Aquarius, every common planetary
nebula is shaped like an hourglass—
remember Time, that wave
that never breaks, but coils
(I mean *curls*) over your head.
Gemini, protect your overhang
and dangly bits. And have a little respect
for money—O, not just its private parts,
but its poor misunderstood soul.
All you bedridden, including those
born with gray hair, keep embarking
on bracing sea voyages.
This particular universe is gas
and rocks—perfect for touring.
Watch for dark powerful wings
flying north at dawn (the reason *belle-*
aurore sounds like *Bellow, roar*!).
Aries, your own bird soul is about to wake.
First one up, start the coffee.
You born today: A little moxie
and good sense, please—
and don't neglect the personal niceties.

THE UNMIXING

All the beavers & exes in attendance & the minister
in rapid-rose silk with a brand new throat button
& all the peoples said Amen & threw thistledown
for the finches to eat & all the ecologists & businessmen

kissed & made up & the earth got hotter & business
got colder until we tasted the nasty stuff & undid it
& hot damn it was hard to sort out Urth's casserole
all those carrots mushroom imps branches of parsley

& lightning goats in heat watery rainbows in our mouths
migrating birds St. George's dragon-killing sword Ascalon
frontispieces backispieces but something higher came
or was it lower & flash floods lashed & cataracts attacked

our upper thighs & everything ended up in the Gulf
of New Mexico or was it Aqaba & the skies looked
like fighting cocks & squid clashing & the sea foamed
with doors swinging open & shut O the shame

of everything turned to slush, heterogeneous turning
homogeneous & vice versa ingenious ingenuous
but hold on hello All over the world it is separating again
Limits & locks on everything but holes & openings too

& even the slowing universe is speeding up because
everyone knows that all that unknown dark matter
& dark energy are just 2 of the multiple hands of me
that quiet fellow pushing you one by one out on the stage

through the painted velvet curtain Most starlight comes
from unseen stars You are no exception & so when we

leave our story the frog I mean the fog has lifted This way
please Out here Yes you Step over the threshold Take some

shape & begin to glow Step lively *Step forward you.*

THE BLUE FLASH

The world, created when I was born,
spewed out, clotting into stars
and valleys. All things appeared

in the afterbirth of that event—
the Air Force, X-files, missing links
waiting to be found, ash-colored

aliens, moustachioed seducers,
urban blight, evolution, the need
to step to a higher level, sex

of course, the expanding spirit,
the first birth, the joy to be found
in hindrance, the jostlings of travel.

Even now, typing this on a May night,
deeps of air erupt into rivulets
rippling outward, groping, growing

into cobalt breakers headed for Tierra
del Fuego, Tasmania, and on to
Paradise. It's a matter of becoming

simple enough to see not just
the green flash, but the rarer
blue flash behind it, straining out

the yellow to see the Blue Man hunched
inside the Green Man, sky-diapered,
sucking his golden thumb, our sun.

ONE FABULOUS BIRD

It was like finding an eland
in Hansel and Gretel,
like turning the moon
into a moron with one small r.
She saw that some loved
the creator and loathed
creation, while some loved creation
and loathed the creator.
Some thought thoughts
were everything, some that
actions were everything.
Some saw truth looming
in the future, others looming

in the past. Some found that
forgiveness brings strength,
some that it wrings all resolve
from the soul. Some held
that evil must be wrestled
into its grave, others that evil
is fused to the good, or at least
pushes the swing that makes
good climb higher. Some act as
God's mastiff or his brass ax.
Others feel that truth lies
all around like dapplings of trees
over a canoe paddled down

a howling river, where owls
and ravens watch and drool,
and an occasional bright woodpecker

bangs his head against a tree
and finds a worm—and where
one bird sometimes soars so high
out of the vast, limitless forest,
that looking down, it sees nothing
but a pig iron goat, a sunken boat,
a fallen wing, a drunken flame,
a culture on a slide, a bit of fluff,
a flake of rust, gust of fever
—puff of dust.

TIME LORD

Full of the round world,
full of the exhausted *luxe*
of remembering and forgetting,
she saw that cheerfulness
and dour fatalism, the hoarding
of dear sorrows, were both
right and proper—two hands,
or more likely, two talons
of the claw of truth.
She half-remembered a song
from a dismembered planet:
I see a new light
On your feathers, Friend.
Don't weep for those
Who fly away on
Owl wings damp with gold.
And yet the dead still lingered
in her skin, buried splinters
which stirred at night.
Remembering the true meaning
of disaster, she cried out,
Bad star! Bad star!
as sunflowers and sunspots
sank beneath her window,
and the moon circled like a wolf.
So what
decreed that beauty attract
its own destruction, that every
nest be torn, every yolk broken?
She was flying through suns
flashing on and off, sparkling
in an overflowing pond—
beautiful, unbearable.

SAILING AT SUNSET

The sunset, first cause
of Plato's perilous tilt toward beauty,
insinuates itself
like a stain across Lake Michigan—
news risen out of Grand Rapids,
motel booked in Sheboygan.

I confess that I too am stung by beauty,
how fair its con, old pro.
But let us not forget Aristotle.

Those three white pines on shore?
All the leaps of your imagination, miscreant,
cannot make them more. French philosophy,
Religious Science, semiotics, cannot make them less.

So what if the sun
drapes himself in apocalyptic plumes, some fancywork
of electrons glittering in the dust.
Those brass knuckles over Milwaukee
are one discrete cloud,
and not all your illimitless universe can make it more.

—Better yet,
give Plato sunrise, the naked flash,
gulls flying agate and porcelain.
Give Aristotle the lake, cooler after the sun goes down—
beauty *in* the lake, not above it.

But remember that this lake, this sailboat, are *blau, bleu, azul,*
even in Sudetenland,
And the mind is more than a posse of changing colors.

At this moment, the cloud-fist listing
                                        leeward toward Chicago,
The Real, like the sun's rays, can be traced to its source.
                    Fresh evidence is always to be found,
                                                my heart-beast,
however it swing and sway, *triste* or *gaie*, in Zwingli time,
                                    toe tapping, table rapping.

Phyllis, keep your mind hard and flat-bellied.
                    Make it a taut bed you can bounce a quarter on.
                                            —And you, anti-Hero,
        who live mortified under the yellow sun (now red),

        fortify your mind with a drop of bitter gravity
                                    to free it from giddiness,
            lusts, gusts, gauds, bawds or flutterings
                            of party-colored birdlets about to spook.

Repeat after me, Three Trees, One Cloud, now a wisp.
Under us, one blue lake, now a field of frothy purple iris.

And throughout, a steady mind—beauty picked up and made
                portable, lilies headed for the honeycomb

—more than the time of day, as the sun
                                    is more than white, yellow or red,
        more than a welder's acetylene torch,
                                    more than a burning zest of lemon,
                more than a sleepy traveler at a Red Roof Inn
                                            sinking into the sheets.

And here comes Night tumbling down on our heads
        like a wooly mammoth

stampeded over a cliff,
uncovering a straggly row
of stern old cave-dwellers' eyes
peering over the rim—
winking back coldly from the lake

—appraising us, taking our measure.

ROWING TO QUINTANA ROO

A red planet mars the sky as I row
my Tipsy Flame deeper into the Gulf,
clouds gathering like choirboys
for evening mass. I've left a heap
of womanish weeps, painted ladies
and red admirals, cute tricks
like Buddhist flutists and nudist lutists,
the family ideology, secret offenses.
I look back at you on shore, one
paw of a sundog glowering over your head,
remembering how often the pomegranate
broke open to spill its collective seeds,
and how only one, stunned, star-split,
magnified into you. Countless lights
cast from your eyes, shoes, belt,
scatter like waterdrops from a faithful geyser,
chips of light from a glitter ball, fireworks
from a tomb, all containers blown
open, spinning with birds feeding, nameless,
spume-driven, in the troughs of waves
—ahead of me, a dizzy moon,
its path fizzing, the mermaid road rising.

Patricia Corbus lives in Sarasota, Florida, where she grew up in her parents' shell shop, The Nautilus.

She graduated from Agnes Scott Collge, holds a Master's degree from the University of North Carolina at Chapel Hill, and an MFA from the Warren Wilson Program for Writers. She has loved poetry for as long as she can remember.